How to Give Just 1 Talk a Month and Fill Up Your Schedule with Patients

Chen Yen

How to Give Just 1 Talk a Month and Fill Up Your Schedule with Patients

Printed by:
90-Minute Books
302 Martinique Drive
Winter Haven, FL 33884
www.90minutebooks.com

Published in the United States of America

Book ID: 170404-00755-2

ISBN-13:978-1643200361
ISBN-10: 1643200364

For more information on 90-Minute Books including how you can publish your own book, visit www.90minutebooks.com or call (863) 318-0464

Disclaimer: Please check with the laws of your state and profession before implementing any marketing ideas in this book.

Here's What's Inside...

I wish I had found yours earlier!
"I had never done a talk before. Within one week, I got booked for my first talk. Within two weeks, I gave it in front of my ideal audience, got clients from it and made $1,000 from it! I had taken other trainings before that were not the right fit for me as an introvert, and wish I found yours earlier!"
—Kathy Mayeda

I have a system I can rely on to get patients.
"I was having a hard time getting people to show up to my talks. After the 6-Figure Speaking Makeover Mentorship for Introverts, I am now getting enough patients for the month by just doing one talk a month. I have a system I can rely on to get patients with. Thank you so much for your guidance and system."
—Melissa M., LAc

My income has doubled following the system.
"I've been in practice for over 12 years and I wanted to work more with nutrition and wellness patients. I followed the 6-Figure Speaking system for Introverts and got booked for 5 talks and have had 50% conversions. Most of my patients from those talks are still here today. Working with Fill My Holistic Practice has been a great experience."
—Dr. David Derosa, DC

Last week I had 8 patients sign up immediately for sessions with me!
"Before working with Chen, my house was on its way to foreclosure--I hit rock bottom and had just moved to a new city to start a practice all over. Within three months of working with Chen, I have made five times the amount of income than I did before. Last week I tried out what Chen teaches, while speaking to a group of 20 individuals at a wellness talk. I have never used this approach in a wellness talk and have been doing wellness talks for the last six years and only received a handful of clients from these talks. Last week I had eight patients sign up immediately for sessions with me! I'm never going back to my old ways! (My house also did not end up going into foreclosure.)"
—Dr. Jannine Krause, ND, LAc

Practical steps and immediate benefits
"I have a 12-year Sports Rehab Chiropractic business. I have already established myself as a rehab specialist and I wanted to expand my services and offer more of my expertise— therefore I reached out to Chen because I saw something in her that I don't see in other Business coaches. I have invested 18K in other business coaches and I am thankful I found Chen."

"Chen has been the most practical, has simple and yet profound useful tips to implement into your practice right away—that is the rare thing I see in Chen. She has propelled me with each call, training or her templates worksheets. I get immediate benefits from working with Chen that I see right away, versus other coaches I didn't see such results."

I have a new way to talk to my clients that gets results.
"I am so glad I've worked with Chen because I have a new way to talk to my clients that gets results. For me, it had me see so many new ways I could just tweak slightly what I was doing and BOOM, results. I have landed clients with a $1,500.00 program that they sell themselves. I don't need to 'talk them into it.".

I got in for a corporate wellness program.
"The 6-Figure Speaking Makeover Mentorship for Introverts, which from just the VIP day alone was hands down the best training to get me started right away. JUST TODAY I had a meeting with a corporation for a corporate wellness program and I know it was from the mentoring from Chen and having everything in place."

...make the biggest difference in your business/life.
"I have referred my colleagues to Chen and they are so thankful I did because Chen's energy and the way she sees into your practice to give you

that special step that can make the biggest difference in your business/life."
—**Dr. Sarah Peters, DC**
Update: Sarah got the corporate contract

I came away with 26 new patients from the talk

"I used to do talks and even though I enjoyed them, people would come up to me and tell me how interesting it was and how it was great information I shared, but it never really brought patients in. I didn't have a good way of monetizing my talks. After using the 6-Figure Speaking System for Introverts and approach, I was able to do a talk in front of 50 people and came away with 26 patients who paid and came to my office for their first visit. I made over $8000 from the talk (which doesn't include the lifetime value of a patient). I feel inspired to do talks, because not only can I educate people about their health issues, but I now have a way of getting patients I can help after the talk."
—**Dr. Kevin Passero, ND, former President of MD Naturopathic Doctors Association**

My rooms are to capacity.

"Before using the 6-Figure Speaking System for Introverts, I had just rented a second room because I wanted to expand. I was a little concerned about being able to generate enough patients. Using the system, I've spoken to three different fertility centers and all three were extraordinarily pleased with how I explained how the acupuncture can integrate with their fertility work. I have the confidence to be able to speak not just about acupuncture in general, but what I bring to the picture. My rooms are to capacity. My practice is booming and I'm thriving personally."

—Lisa Grant, LAc.

Introduction

Do you wish it were easier to get patients in the door? Whenever you're busy with patients, you love it. Your patients also love you. But you feel disappointed about having gaps in your schedule. Some days are really busy and you feel validated with what you're doing, but then it slows down. You go back to worrying about how to get more patients in. As a result, the constant unpredictability about the practice feels stressful.

Another possibility is that you might feel burnt out. Your practice is busy. You always seem to have something to do and there's never enough time in the day. Associates or other practitioners may be a part of your practice and you want them to be busier.

When was the last time you were able to take a vacation without having to think twice about it and being concerned that your patients weren't taken care of? It would be nice to take time off while money is coming in, without you having to always be there to make sure everything happens.

Speaking is one of the fastest ways to fill your practice. You can show up, do a talk on a topic you are passionate about, and get more patients in one hour than you would from a whole month of networking, if you know what you're doing. Speaking is also a great way to reach more people at once and educate people about their healthcare options.

If you are busy enough and don't want more patients, imagine if you had a way to make a bigger impact by monetizing your expertise beyond seeing patients 1-on-1. I'm going to be showing you a way you can set things up so you can even be at a beach somewhere while money is still coming in the door. You can be "speaking" and educating many people without getting dressed up for it.

Enjoy the book!

I hope it changes the way you think about speaking and encourages you to start or speak more to wake up the planet!

To your success!

Chen Yen

The 6-Figure Speaking System for Introverts

I started my career working as a pharmacist on Native American reservations. I enjoyed the adventure of traveling to different reservations, getting to know the tribes, their culture, and working with the Native Americans. Soon, though, I started hating going to work every day. I remember one Groundhog Day clearly in the pharmacy. As I filled yet another prescription for Prozac and handed it to a woman at the counter, I felt angry. I wasn't angry at her, but angry at what our healthcare system was putting in front of her.

It was as if that were the only option she had and I was endorsing it. The truth was I didn't take medications myself. I felt like a hypocrite handing out pills day in and day out, especially when giving them out like candy was far outside my own belief system. For example, my sister and I rarely took medications as children. Whenever I had a cough or sore throat, my mom would open the cabinet and give us Chinese herbal syrup. Whenever we were sick with a cold, we just slept more and got better on our own.

Unfortunately, what I observed working in a pharmacy was vastly different from that. Little kids would come to the clinic for immunization shots and leave with a little cocktail of medications, including Tylenol, even when they weren't hurting from the shot anymore. Adults with chronic issues would often be given 10–20 medications as if they were harmless like candy and not a big deal at all.

Some providers I worked with were open minded. However, some acted like they knew everything. It was apparent they didn't know everything because patients did not have answers to their health issues.

The thought of our future generation of healthcare providers in the traditional medical model also concerned me. For example, I can still remember a pharmacy student doing a rotation at our pharmacy, making fun of homeopathy. The topic somehow came up and he said to me with extreme conviction: "That homeopathic stuff is bogus. Do people really think that stuff works? It has practically nothing in it." He wasn't interested in exploring the science behind it and wrote it off as bogus because he didn't understand it.

It drove me crazy. I felt frustrated contributing to a system which didn't help people get well. Even though I was well paid in my job, I couldn't fully stand up for what I really believed in by staying stuck in that soul-depriving environment.

I finally hit a wall and decided, "I can't live like this. I have to get out." I didn't know what to do next, though. Other pharmacists around me were unhappy and counting down towards retirement from their government jobs. With the limited clarity I had at that point in time, I decided to help other pharmacists get into more fulfilling jobs, because I still saw the need for acute medications. Fast forward five years, I had started and grown a successful recruiting business from zero to seven figures.

I used to always think, as long as I made more money and could do what I wanted to outside of my professional life, I'd be happy. I thought I would feel like I "made it" when I made seven figures. But once I made seven figures, things started to break down. A lot of struggle started to show up in different aspects of my life. My business started to stagnate. I tried to work harder to grow it more, but I also noticed a part of me kept sabotaging the growth. I didn't want to admit it then, but I couldn't see myself growing the business more significantly because my heart wasn't totally in it.

I had a choice. I could either keep doing what I was doing and make a great living or face that something needed to change. It took months of soul searching until I realized what I needed to do was stop pretending. I stopped pretending it was okay I was still primarily selling my soul to help people get on medications. All the while, I was into holistic things such as acupuncture, energy work, seeking enlightenment spiritually, not taking any medications, and not owning a cell phone. It was as if I had a secret life I couldn't keep to myself any longer.

I was tired of seeing people mainly being prescribed drugs and thinking they were getting the care they needed. It's time for our healthcare system to be truly integrated, so it's not just about drugs, surgery, and sick care. Imagine people having the best of both worlds—our traditional medical model which is fantastic with acute care, surgery, and certain aspects of diagnosing, plus holistic options which are effective for prevention and resolving conditions at the root cause. More and more people are interested in options outside of our conventional healthcare system, but this movement towards holistic health is not happening quickly enough. The problem is people don't know about you or do they understand what you do.

We cannot leave it up to our government to change things. We cannot leave it up to insurance companies to change things. It starts with holistic health practitioners like you getting the word out about holistic options which get to the root of a lot of health conditions. You are the ones who can lead the change in this movement, but people need to know about you.

Speaking is one of the fastest ways to educate and inspire people, so they realize there are other effective options available to them. Speaking is one of the fastest ways to educate other providers that what you do is not just woo-woo, non-scientific, and ineffective.

Now that you have read my story, you might be thinking, "Well, that's an interesting story, but what does your growing a seven-figure recruiting business have to do with my getting patients more predictably by speaking?"

Having come from the traditional medical model, there are things I see which you may not be seeing about growing your practice. For example, how to get your foot in the door for untapped opportunities, including getting "in" to speak in front of other providers so more patient referrals come to you.

I'm an introvert. When it came to marketing my business, I would often find myself procrastinating. I would beat myself up for not doing the things my extroverted mentors told me I needed to do to grow my business. I used to think something was wrong with me. Networking seemed to be so easy for other people, but it would exhaust me. I would often have to force myself to do those things.

I was always looking for a more effective way to grow my business without having to always put myself out there. Quite honestly, I used to dread speaking. I grew up in a strict family: a first generation immigrant family from Taiwan. I remember being eight years old. Every Sunday morning when the newspaper would come was one of my most dreaded moments. I used to imagine how other kids would probably get excited about being able to read the comic strips in the Sunday paper. I was jealous of them. For me, I felt a sense of dread and anxiety, because Sunday morning papers meant I would need to do a current event talk in front of my dad.

My dad was very strict. He was a PhD research scientist and a materials science engineer with a dry, rigid style of speaking. He would critique me to the point of crying and it gave me extreme anxiety. I used to believe I would never speak in front of an audience if given the choice, because it gave me so much performance anxiety.

There was, however, a part of me who loved to teach. That led me to learn from mentors who showed me how to do talks to inspire people and get clients from it. That development of my skill with speaking led me to have five-figure months within the first year of my second business and multi-six figures within a couple of years.

It's a system my holistic health practitioners learn from; it comes from my experience of speaking and from what I have learned and observed from my mentors.

My clients often experience 40–60%+ conversions using the 6-Figure Speaking System for Introverts. For example, the skill of 40% conversions results in 8 new patients when speaking in front of an audience of 20 people. I'm really excited to be sharing nuggets from the system with you, as those things have allowed me to be able to travel to the Himalayas, go on spiritual trips, to enjoying homestays in Fiji and rich experiences in the Dominican Republic. Traveling where you want to when you want is something you will be able to do when you master this and have a system in place which gives you predictability. It is also a powerful and effective way to share what you know with more people, so you can help more people who need you.

Why Speak?

One of the most challenging things about having your own practice is getting new patients in the door. People don't know about you. If other holistic health practitioners are doing similar work as you, how will people decide to come to you instead of someone else?

Another challenge is people not understanding exactly what you do. Do you cringe when you hear people say things like, "Oh, I don't like getting my back cracked", because that's all they think a chiropractor does? Or "Don't those needles hurt?", if you're an acupuncturist?

When you speak, you will be able to be seen as a go-to expert very quickly. Instead of reaching one person at a time, it could be one to many—1 to 10, 1 to 50, 100, or more. You may even be at a stage in your business that stage where it makes sense for you to do a webinar, and you don't even need to leave your house to do that. You could be reaching hundreds or thousands of people all at the same time.

Paid Speaking or Free?

Let's start by looking at the different opportunities you have to make money speaking. As a speaker, you can consider doing either paid talks or free talks. Paid opportunities are nice because you know you will get paid for it even before you do the talk. For example, you could be speaking for professional associations, organizations, or conferences. There are local or national ones which pay for speaking. Examples are health care professional conferences, HR conferences, etc. Typically, larger venues offer more paid opportunities.

Other opportunities to speak are in front of potential patients. For example, one of my clients is a holistic MD who works with kids with autism issues. There's an annual autism conference parents and kids with autism attend. It's a national conference which includes speakers as part of its activities.

How much can you expect to get paid?
Some talks pay a couple hundred dollars and cover the conference registration fee. You can get paid even more; thousands of dollars or more for keynoting. Even if you are not a professional speaker, you can keynote for talks. In fact, conferences are looking for fresh motivational topics which can be beneficial for their audience.

Other kinds of paid opportunities include speaking at corporations. Did you know corporations pay for lunch-and-learns? It could be $1,000. Many times, chiropractors do lunch-and-learns for free for corporations. But that is not necessary. It is possible to get paid to do them if you know how to command what you would like to charge.

Beyond the talk itself, it is possible to offer corporate wellness programs. For example, a health coach offered five-week nutrition based corporate wellness program to a corporation and charged several thousand dollars for it. He worked with the employees of the company by phone in a group setting.

A chiropractor client of mine got her foot in the door with a company and was able to work with the executives of the company. She not only offered chiropractic but also another modality. The company paid her for it. On top of that, she ended up getting patients from that experience, because some of the executives ended up learning about her and trusting her enough to become her patient.

What are other paid opportunities?
There are paid speaking opportunities at universities and colleges. Did you know that university groups and departments have budgets for speakers, including those who speak on

health-related topics? Sometimes what you offer doesn't even have to just be a talk. For example, one health coach got paid several thousand dollars to do a cooking demonstration for a few hours at a university health center. As a holistic health practitioner, you could talk about topics related to your expertise or nutrition to students and get paid for it. Those are just a few of the opportunities to making money with paid talks.

The drawback about paid talks is they usually require more of a vetting process to "get in" with. Expect to experience typically a longer decision-making process (than if you are doing free talks), because the company or organization is paying out of pocket for it. You may experience competition for paid opportunities. Also, most organizations willing to pay for someone to speak are looking for people with experience speaking.

What about free talks?
Free talks are great because you can set up a free talk in a week, give a talk, and come away with patients or clients from it. If you do a free talk for an organization, it's easier to "get in" because they are free. When you know how to structure your free talk, you can easily make money from it. It doesn't matter whether it's a free talk or a paid speaking opportunity. When you get a paid speaking gig, the money from it can be extra gravy. It can be enjoyed as double-dipping.

Now that you have a better sense of some of the avenues where you can get paid speaking, let's have look at how you can speak and then walk away with new patients. One way is to speak for the purpose of educating people and inspiring people to book appointments with you. You can either host your own talks or speak in front of other people's audiences. The nice part about hosting your own talks is you can set one up quickly, even within a week, and do the talk. If you host a talk at your clinic, people have the opportunity to experience your surroundings. They're more likely to feel comfortable with you and the environment. The disadvantage is you need to organize it and inspire people to show up.

Another option is to speak in front of other people's audiences, such as groups or organizations. The nice part about that is when you speak you are immediately seen as an expert simply because you're the guest speaker. You also don't need to do the legwork of filling up your own talks. You just need to get your foot in the door to speak, and all you need to do is show up for it. The host does the legwork of filling up the talks.

Instead of doing talks in front of potential patients, you can speak in front of potential referrers. Have you ever considered speaking in front of other providers who could be sending you referrals? For example, you could be speaking to a roomful of other health care providers. Instead of being in front of a potential patient who might become a patient him/herself and perhaps refer a patient, if you spoke in front of a provider, you could be getting patient referrals. Imagine if you had one MD or other provider send you two referrals a week. Imagine if you had three MDs sending you two referrals a week. What would that do for your practice?

At some point, a snowball effect happens and you won't even need to do as many talks. For example, a chiropractor client of mine got her foot in the door in front of an MD who is also an ND. We mapped out what she was going to say, down to details of what she was going to bring. Now she's getting referrals from that provider and she hasn't really had to do more presentations in front of her.

When you speak in front of other providers, the presentation can be in front of just a single provider or can be in a roomful of providers.

An acupuncturist client of mine spoke in front of an MD office recently where several MDs attended, along with their staff. The whole office was excited about the talk. The day of the talk, the office staff was trying to figure out where to put my client's materials up in the office. The day after, she received a referral from a doctor. Now her practice is at full capacity just by getting "in" with three MD offices.

If you would like to be successful with this, you'll need to have an approach that works to get your foot in the door so the doctors give you the time of day. Then you'll need to have a special talk created just for providers. It is different from a typical presentation you might expect to give at a clinical conference to providers. It is one thing for doctors to feel like you know a lot; it's another thing for them to think of you first to send you patients consistently.

After the talk, there are certain things to have in place so they remember you and think of you first to send patients to when the need arises. But imagine just doing this a few times. You could be set with a consistent flow of patients if you know what you're doing.

Become a Hub for Your Community
The third approach of speaking and doubling your patient base (or more!) is to consider "How can I actually be a hub in my community?" Especially if you host talks in your own office and have been disappointed by the turnout, consider approaching speaking with a fresh perspective.

Instead of looking at it as, "I'm hosting this one talk at my office," start considering your clinic as a hub in your community where people can come to for holistic health education. Imagine if your clinic is the place people think of and go to for that. Your clinic could be *the* place in your community where people get educated about different holistic options by you and by other holistic health practitioners.

To give you an example, one of my clients is a chiropractor and a naturopathic physician who started her own practice. Having trouble finding patients, she decided to start giving talks but her engagements weren't converting her audience to patients. Out of an audience of 40, she was experiencing only a 3% conversion rate. After we worked together, she ended up experiencing 25 to 40% conversion rate.

At the end of three months, she quadrupled her income. One thing which used to disappoint her was she would hold talks at her office, but hardly anyone would show up. After we started working together, she ended up experiencing standing room only at each of her talks. How did she do that? She invited other practitioners to the talk and had them invite their patients to it.

One thing we also discussed was reaching out to the providers to invite them to donate a raffle prize to the talk if they had an interest in doing so. This allowed the provider to get more exposure without having to do extra work. It gave the audience an opportunity to understand that provider's services more. It also inspired those practitioners to invite their patient base to the talk because they became more on board with collaborating together.

My client was able to reach more people than she typically reached from her talks that day. She brought in more patients from that talk than she did before without having to do a lot of additional marketing. She was also able to start developing a relationship with the providers she reached out to.

Have you ever tried to reach out to other providers with the attempt to develop a mutual referral relationship, but never heard back? It can be discouraging. If you have someone in mind you'd like to start developing a relationship with, one effective approach is to invite that practitioner to speak at your clinic; then offer to speak at *his/her* clinic. This allows both of you to collaborate and educate both of your communities with your individual areas of expertise. It benefits both of you because you're able to reach a bigger audience than you would have on your own.

Does this start giving your ideas to think bigger? These are some ideas from the 6-Figures Speaking System for Introverts. You don't have to always be doing the hard work of marketing, spending money advertising, and feeling disappointed. Consider how to reach more people at once so it is a better use of your time.

How to Leverage Your Time Beyond Seeing Patients 1-on-1

There are ways you can leverage your talks beyond just bringing in more patients one-on-one. From your talk, you can encourage people to come in and book an appointment or have an initial exam. What else could you offer from your talk that could really help people?

One thing you could consider doing is offering a treatment plan or package straight from the talk, if it's appropriate and helpful to the client. For example, a chiropractor client of mine who has been helping people lose weight (and noticing many diabetics' HgA1C go down), offers a $1,500 package straight from the talk. The last talk he did, he experienced over 70% conversions straight from the talk, meaning 70% of the audience moved forward with the package he offered. As a result of the talk he did, he was able to help the people who signed up and were excited about care. What he noticed later was these people were more committed to their care than if they had just come in visit by visit. Because of that, they also got better results because they were more compliant with care. In the end, this led to higher patient satisfaction and more referrals.

Have you ever given a talk before where you encouraged people to book an initial consult or exam, but even though they signed up, they didn't show up in your office afterwards? This will happen less frequently when you offer a package straight from the talk. People would be interested in taking you up on it if it makes sense and what you offer is valuable.

One common approach to this is to give people a discount for a series of treatments, but it doesn't have to be the only approach when offering packages. There are other approaches to offering a treatment or package so you don't feel resentful that you are taking a pay cut whenever you are offering packages. For example, decide first, "Hmm, what could I put together that can really help my patient with the desired outcomes I want them to have?" For example, is there any part of what you do which could be done in a group setting? This is especially perfect for those of you who have branched out with nutrition or functional medicine. You could host some group health coaching calls instead of all individual sessions; it can leverage your time.

It can also be valuable for the people you help. For example, in many situations, proper nutrition can actually help your patients/clients get to their desired health outcomes faster.

The challenge is lasting change doesn't happen from just a short verbal reminder during visits. It requires them making lifestyle changes which can be hard to make if they are trying to do it on their own.

If you provided a structure to support transformation, your patients or clients are more likely to be successful. You can create accountability structures such as group calls which allow for people to be supported by each other and by you.

This concept is not just limited to nutrition or functional medicine either. I have a naturopathic physician client of mine who helps people who have been diagnosed with cancer. Many patients diagnosed with cancer could really benefit from receiving support from someone they can talk to aside from just family members or friends. When someone is diagnosed with cancer, there is a lot to think about; treatment options and life decisions, plus different challenges mentally, emotionally, and sometimes financially. Doctors, nurses, family members, and friends can only help to some extent, because they understand it through their perspective only. Imagine those patients having the support of others through the same thing without having to leave their house. That's what group calls can do for them.

What can you charge for offering packages?
I have seen packages offered between $197 and $3000 dollars or even more. It depends on what you are offering, the level of access to you, and your expertise. Of course, be within the laws of your state and profession with regulations.

Aside from offering things that help with patient care, you can offer educational products or programs. Do you ever say the same things over and over again to your patients? Sometimes you may feel like a broken record. Even so, patients don't always remember the advice, even if it has been given to them more than once.

What if you could put that information into a program or a product that is helpful, plus get paid for it? You could charge between $97 and $997 for it. Just to give you an example, one health coach offered a five-week online group detox program and charged $197 dollars for it. She had more than 150 people in the program. Do the math. 150 x $197 = $29,550 (and that doesn't include what she made from the supplements). She offered five group calls which were essentially five hours of her time. That's essentially getting paid $5910/hr. There was no private time with her. In fact, you had to pay extra for private time if you wanted it. She also offered her own line of supplements which helped with the detoxing. Everyone paid extra for it if they wanted it.

After the group detox program, she offered a gut rebuilding program online. That was the area of expertise she enjoyed the most. She offered a group program which was essentially once a month calls and a couple of videos a month for several months. She had more than 100 people in it. Do the math. 100 x $997 = $99,700.

People were happy with the programs. I know because I was a part of both programs. I saw the many positive posts and comments in our private Facebook page. People were pleased with it.

You might wonder how she filled up her group programs. It was by doing talks, both in-person talks and webinars. When you have a talk which not only educates but also inspires people to work with you further, you can do this too.

Does this give you some ideas about what you could be doing to leverage your time and allow you to help people beyond just seeing patients one-on-one?

Think about your services, what are additional possibilities to expand your reach, help more people at once, and bring another stream of revenue into your practice?

For example, if you have figured something out which is working well for you in your own practice, you can train other health care providers on it. It could be on your special technique/approach of treating patients, or effective office/marketing systems that work. Imagine helping other providers become more successful in their practices and creating a ripple effect throughout the country and even the world? You can offer on-demand (home study) training or online group programs. You can charge $497, $997, and even more than that, and even host the programs by phone so you don't have to leave the house.

You can literally be on a beach somewhere, host a call, and then go back to your relaxing on the beach. You can also offer group classes or workshops in person if you prefer that kind of interaction.

How Speaking Can Lead to Passive Income

Speaking can also be an avenue to bring in passive income while helping more people. Trading time for money can only go so far, because money doesn't come in when you're not there and actively involved. If you have a passive income stream, however, money can be coming in even when you are on vacation or spending time with your family.

There are different kinds of passive income opportunities available. Could you explore further into opportunities you believe in and that you feel can help your patients? For example, there are companies that offer high quality essential oils which can be made available to your patients. You can also make money by introducing other people to the essential oils you love.

One common challenge when you have an interest like this is having enough time in the day to network with people and educate them about it. Instead of feeling like you have to always be networking with people one-on-one to spark interest, you could instead do one talk in front of 20 people and educate them about it. Once people are more informed and understand what you are offering, they will be excited to be on board if it resonates with them.

Another possibility is offering supplements which can be beneficial to people. The challenge is there are many supplements on the market and people don't know what to take or what brand to use. Quality and storage practices are variable depending on the source. Most holistic health practitioners have researched and have access to quality supplements. If people are educated about supplements, they will understand the benefit of getting supplements from a health care provider instead of a random store. You could make available an online store that people may purchase supplements and other health products from which you may introduce during your talks.

You could also offer services beneficial to other providers. For example, a client of mine is a naturopathic physician. He brings in more than half a million dollars a year having a practice that's just himself with the support of his front office staff. He only works three days a week. The reason he is bringing in a good amount of money is he also has a passive income stream from private labeling supplements. One challenge patients encounter is getting access to quality supplements at a good price. My client ended up going direct to manufacturers and started manufacturing high quality supplements to make available to his patients. In addition, he offers other practitioners the opportunity to private label those high-quality supplements. Other providers are able to access to high quality supplements for their patients; they also are able to bring in a source of revenue from the markup of the supplements.

It is also a way for my client to make passive income from offering private labeling to those providers. When my client first reached out to me, he wanted to expand the passive income side of his practice. We did that by getting a talk in place to educate practitioners on the benefits of private labeling supplements and increase the number of practitioners on board with it.

Speaking Pays!

Let's work out some numbers here. Let's just say you're speaking in front of 50 people and you just offered an initial consultation or exam for $150 dollars from your talk. If you got your conversions up to 40% from your talk, that would be 20 new patients from one hour of your time. How many talks like that would you need to fill up your practice? You'd also be bringing in $3000 from the talk. That doesn't even take into account the revenue from the follow up visits or the lifetime value of a patient. Also, 40% conversions is on the lower end for many of my clients using the 6-Figure Speaking System for Introverts. My clients are typically converting on average between 40% and 60% from their talks when the immediate offer is something which is a couple of hundred dollars or less.

Another possibility is what Dr. C. Barnes did. When she first came to me, she had made $500 that month and still had to borrow money from her parents. She had worked for another practice before and then started a practice of her own. She wanted to work primarily with women who are pregnant and their kids when they were born. But she was having a hard time getting patients. It just wasn't what she thought it would be. She thought it would be faster to start up her practice.

In three months after using the 6-Figure Speaking System for Introverts, Dr. Barnes brought in $5000 a month in her practice and it has continuously grown since. Her conversions from talks went from 0 to 60% conversions. In the end, she began offering packages from her talks.

As we mentioned earlier, what if you offered packages from your talks? Like my other chiropractor client Bill does; the one I shared with you earlier. He charges $1,500 for his packages. He just experienced 70% conversions from a recent talk. But let's be conservative here. If you're in front of 20 people and offered a package for $1500, and experienced 40 percent conversions; that would be $12,000 from a one-hour talk. It's perfect for you if you don't want to be out there all the time marketing. This is possible for you even if you are an acupuncturist, naturopathic physician, or holistic MD. Providers in different professions are doing this; it's not limited to chiropractors.

The Biggest Mistakes Holistic Health Practitioners Make When Trying to Get More Patients by Speaking

You have learned several ways to get paid by speaking. Now let's discuss the biggest mistakes many holistic health practitioners make when doing talks which keep them from getting patients. The two most common frustrations are that either few people show up to self-hosted talks, or it's challenging to get booked for talks. A lot of effort can go into hosting a talk, including handing out flyers and telling people about it. Sometimes few people end up coming and it's discouraging.

Another way is to try to get booked in the community, but a common challenge is getting a foot in the door with speaking opportunities. Not hearing back can feel frustrating and lead to wanting to give up.

Another common issue is getting patients or clients from talks. Have you ever experienced people coming up to you after a talk and saying, "That was a great talk. Thanks!" But few patients come from it. It is exciting to feel a high when giving the talk, but nothing comes of it. Maybe you have even handed out business cards before and people say they are going to call you, but days or weeks later, you don't hear from them. It's disappointing. It starts to feel like too much free public service after a while. People are also not getting the help they really need. Most people do not all of a sudden just get better from coming to listening to a talk. They get better from the care you can provide them.

Let's look at each of these issues and address them. How to actually get people to show up? You need to have a system for filling up your own talks or getting booked elsewhere. The second thing is to have a signature talk in place you can use over and over again, and one that actually brings in patients. It is one thing to just do a talk and be informative; it is another to have a talk which not only educates but also inspires patients to come in the door.

One of my clients, Dave, used to get patients from his talks, but was experiencing only 10% conversions in recent years. He was also having trouble getting booked. He had a successful practice but felt like he had reached a ceiling in his practice. Dave had been with a lot of other practice management companies over the years, but the approaches never completely resonated for him as an introvert. After the 6-Figure Speaking Makeover Mentorship for Introverts, his income doubled within a few months. One of the things which contributed to his income doubling so quickly was he got booked for five talks very quickly and started experiencing 30 to 50% conversions, which is a lot higher than he was experiencing most recently.

Let me share with you a couple of things from the 6-Figure Speaking System for Introverts which allowed him, all of a sudden, to get booked for a handful of talks very quickly.

The first step is to get booked for talks or fill up your own talks (Get Booked Formula). The second step is to create a signature talk which brings in patients (design your "Clients Come to Me" Signature Talk).

The first thing to look at is what is the biggest reason people aren't coming? One of the most overlooked reasons is the topic and the title of your talk. We might think we are speaking about a great topic, but is it really all that interesting to people? Who you attract to your talk can also be a reason new patients are not coming in from it.

For example, here are a few titles I have seen people speak on: "Achieving Health through Chiropractic", "Nutrition 101", or "10 Steps to Good Health". What is the problem with these titles? Part of the problem with these kinds of topics is it isn't addressing a "$1,000 problem". What is a "$1,000 problem"? It is an urgent, pressing, and expensive daily struggle people are dealing with. What is an expensive, urgent, daily struggle kind of problem people are dealing with? Do you have a talk topic related to that?

Most people don't care about general topics like achieving health or wellness through chiropractic, acupuncture, or naturopathic medicine. Even if they care, the topic may not be interesting enough to inspire them to get off the couch and drive 30 minutes each way to come and hear your talk. Most people care about the issue(s) or challenges they are having right now which has been bothering them. People are also more likely to do something about their situation when it is a pressing issue.

Your talk needs to address their "$1,000 problem". If you even just tweak this one thing, it can help you with getting more people who are ready to do something about their health to your talks. You're more likely to get patients that way. Then you just need to have the right signature talk angle and content which helps attract the patients you want to come to your practice.

Are you curious about what areas to work on so that more patients come in from your talks? Take the Speak and Get Patients Factor Quiz now:
www.OneTalkaMonthBook.com/quiz

Design an Eye-Catching Talk Title

The next step of the Get Booked Formula is to design your eye-catching talk title. Have you ever attended a conference, opened up the conference agenda and had to decide which talk to attend? Maybe you looked at all the talk titles and thought, "Oh that sounds boring. Let me go to this other one instead." Or maybe a title caught your attention and you thought, "This looks like a really interesting talk, I'm going to go to that!" If a talk title is not eye catching and interesting, people may not come to the talk simply because of the title.

How can you create a talk title that is interesting?

Let me give an example of some things to think about when coming up with a talk title, so people who are ready for what you offer will be more likely to show up to your talk. Speaking can feel like a lot of effort for little results when you're not in front of the right people. But if you are speaking in front of the right audience, you will attract more patients from your talks.

Let me give you something straight from the 6-Figures Speaking System for Introverts. This is from Get Booked Formula part of the system— the template you can use to create your eye-catching talk title. Here are a couple of tips you can think about as you create your title.

Bring up a controversial or fresh perspective in your title. For example, "Nutrition 101" or "How to Lose Weight without Dieting" is not a controversial or fresh perspective. There are many talks about losing weight. That topic may have been fresh years ago when the concept of losing weight without dieting was a newer concept. But now it is a common topic.

If you can bring a fresh perspective to losing weight in the title, more people will be likely to show up. One example is "What Hormones Have to Do with Losing Weight, and How to Lose it Without Yo-Yo Dieting or another Fad Diet". Or "3 Overlooked Reasons to Having Trouble Losing Weight and How to Lose it Without Yo-Yo Dieting or another Fad Diet".

Another tip is to use a number in the title. Why a number? People are busy these days. If people feel they are going to be getting something very tangible from the talk, they are more likely to show up. Studies have been done on this. Odd numbers are better than even numbers. Numbers like 3, 5, and 7 are better than even numbers. Ideally use a number lower than 10, because it can start to feel overwhelming if over ten different concepts are covered in a talk.

Include a phrase in your title which is eye catching. A few title ideas from the template: "3 overlooked ways to...", or "natural approaches to…" Other words to consider using are: "increased, reduced, effective way, easier, or proven". For example, "3 things about [INSERT YOUR TOPIC] many doctors won't tell you."

Let me share with you an example of one of my acupuncturist clients and what happened with her title. Before, she had a hard time getting people on board for packages. She was experiencing 20% conversions from her talks when we first started working together. Now, she has experienced up to 50% of the audience committing to working with her in the capacity of a $2,000 package straight from the talk. She just does one talk a month and is busy enough with that. She sent me a note by email recently and she said, "I can't think about getting more patients right now because I'm so busy with what I'm already doing."

One of the early successes she had was filing up her talks with more qualified people. Her title originally had "Facial Rejuvenation Acupuncture" in it. The problem with that is most people don't know what that exactly means and why they would want it. We tweaked her title and she started advertising her talk with her new title. Two weeks before the talk, she had more people sign-up than ever before.
Why did it end up attracting more of her ideal patients to the talk and why is she converting more often from it? One key factor was changing

the title of her talk from "Facial Rejuvenation Acupuncture" to "Beyond Botox: The Safe, Natural, and Effective Way to Get Rid of Bags, Sags, and Wrinkles." "Beyond Botox" is likely attracting someone who is probably considering or already using Botox. If that's the case, those people are more likely going to want facial rejuvenation acupuncture. Notice the words used in the talk title: "to get rid of bags, sags, and wrinkles". Facial rejuvenation acupuncture isn't what people tend to think they need. But getting rid of bags under the eyes or wrinkles is what people would tend to want for themselves.

Those are some things to really look at; especially the detail of the right talk title can make a big difference, even down to the details of what would be exactly the title which will attract the most ideal kinds of patients to you. Not just anyone, but your ideal kinds of patients.

The Best Places to Get Booked for Speaking

Let's talk about the second step in the process. The first step is to create a talk title that's eye-catching before you even do anything—before you spend money on advertising, before you market your talk or try to get booked. The second step of the 6-Figures Speaking System for Introverts is to decide the best places to get booked. Sometimes the tendency is to just think, "I can get in front of this audience pretty easily, so I'm going to speak in front of them."

For example, you may have considered speaking at gyms, or libraries, or places like Whole Foods. But are those really the best places to be speaking, or are there better places? This is really important strategically. This is the second key to getting patients predictably from your talks. Carefully evaluate where to get booked. Its importance is not to be overlooked.

The first question to ask yourself before deciding to say "yes" to any speaking opportunity is, "Am I in front of 100% of my most ideal kinds of patients or clients?" Why consider thinking this way? Of course, it's not totally black and white 100%, but thinking in this way will give you a strong visual to make sound decisions.
For example, if you're wanting to fish for fish, would you rather fish out of a pond full of fish, or

would you rather fish out of a pond full of turtles, snakes, frogs, ducks, and fish? My guess is a pond full of fish. That is the same exact thing to consider when deciding what to say yes to with speaking opportunities.

Would you like some ideas for where the best places are to be speaking? Let me give you the Top 10 Best Places to Speak and Get Patients Quickstart Guide. That will give you a list of places to speak that can be an effective use of time when wanting to inspire patients or clients to come in from talks. Download it now at: **www.onetalkamonthbook.com/quickstart**.

In summary, you learned about the second step and how it is important to be strategic and selective about who you are speaking in front of.

Fill Up Your Talks

The third step is to get your foot in the door to get booked, or to fill up your own talks. You might be doing talks in your own office right now. But what if you could actually do talks elsewhere? If you do talks elsewhere, the nice part is you don't have to do the legwork of marketing your talk. You don't have to do the leg work of paying for advertising or spending all that effort trying to get people's attention to show up to it. Just show up, do the talk, and get seen as a go-to expert by the audience simply by being the guest speaker. If you would like to get invited to speak, it's important to first be able to get your foot in the door, so places know about you.

Have you ever tried to reach out to places to get booked, but people didn't end up calling back? When you don't hear back, you may start wondering, "What do I do? Should I call them? But I don't want to hassle them."

When you have some key things in place, it will be a lot easier to get booked quickly. For example, a client of mine had never been booked for talks before. Within a week after following the system on how exactly how to get her foot in the door, she ended up getting booked for a talk right away. In two weeks, she got booked for another talk. If that can happen for a total newbie, then it can happen for you, too.

One thing which is really important to have is a good speaker one sheet. A compelling speaker one sheet will help you get taken more seriously as a speaker. It's essentially your business card as a speaker. Many holistic health practitioners don't have one, or haven't thought about getting one created. But if you have one and it's compelling, you will stand out. Places will be more likely to book you.

It also needs to be strategic. When I work with my clients, we are very specific about what to include, what not to include, and in what order. For example, I recently shared with my clients one specific thing to add to their speaker one sheet and it's resulting in patients coming in even when people don't actually show up to the talk.

Get a speaker one sheet in place. Then have a process for determining which opportunities to pursue or not. If you are doing talks at your own office, have a system for filling up your own talks. Some things work better than paying money to advertise.

For example, a chiropractor friend of mine grew two successful multi-six-figure chiropractic practices and sold them. Part of the reason the buyer bought his recent practice is because he had a system for getting people to come to his office talks. He had reached a point in his practice where he would do talks in his office after work and walk away with $10k paydays from his talks.

It wasn't always that way. Back when he started doing talks, he had heard that doing talks could be a great way to educate people and get patients, so he started doing them in his office. But sometimes only two or three people would show up. He started to wish people wouldn't show up so he wouldn't have to do the talk. Then he figured out an effective way to get people to show up to his talks. One main approach he used was Meetup. He created his own Meetup group and started inviting people to his talks. It continued to gain momentum as more and more people came. Of course, you need to know what you are doing. Just simply starting a Meetup group is not enough.

Here's something you can use right away to get more people to come to the talks you host. It's an overlooked approach to fill up your talks more, especially if you have patients in your practice. Ask your patients (or people you know) to invite people to come. How you ask makes a difference in whether more people come. Here is a script from the 6-Figure Speaking System for Introverts:

"As a patient of mine, I wanted to keep you in the loop about something that's coming up / that you're invited to.

"A lot of people with _____ [INSERT HEALTH ISSUE] are not getting better with _____ [INSERT CURRENT WAY OF TREATING ISSUE]. They feel _____ [INSERT HOW THEY'RE FEELING]

"Something that is missing from the current way of treating _____ [INSERT HEALTH ISSUES] is _____. I'm doing a talk on _____. Can you think of one or two people who have _____ [INSERT HEALTH ISSUE] who may want to know about this?"

Use a system which works to get people to show up to the talks. For example, a lot of your success with this is in the details. Especially if you are thinking to yourself, "I've tried that before and it didn't work". It's actually the details which will allow you to actually get patients more predictably. There are templates and scripts you can get for things like this.

Why Some Talks Don't Bring in Patients

Now you've learned the first big problem many people have when doing talks to try to get patients. That is to actually get people to show up or to get booked for talks. The second most common problem is, people love the talk but don't come into the practice from it. Here are the most common biggest mistakes in the talk which could be the reason people aren't coming into your practice afterwards.

One common mistake is getting too much into the clinical side of things. It is how many of us are trained and how we are used to communicating. As clinicians, we've been trained to talk so we come across intelligently. But the problem is, if you're including a lot of big words like subluxation, MTHFR, liver chi stagnation, it starts sounding like Russian to someone who is hearing for the first time what you're talking about.

What are you saying in your talks right now? Is it too clinical? Is it making people fall asleep? You may be losing people because it's over their head.

Another big mistake is including too much information in your talk. As holistic health practitioners, many of us are natural givers.

We like to give and give. However, too much information can make people feel "full", and when people are "full", they don't tend to take action because they are still processing all the information you've just dumped on them.

Instead, there's an art and a skill to having a fine balance of those elements above in your talk, because you definitely want to be educating people. You don't want it to be just general information either. You want your talk to be very engaging, interesting, and stay at their level. Keep that in mind as you create your talk.

Next, does your talk inspire people to take that next step without you being too pushy or salesy, or without being awkward about it? Have you ever attended a talk before which you enjoyed, but then all of a sudden, it got to the end where it just felt like the speaker went into sales mode and you felt so icky and turned off by it? You didn't like that feeling and you don't want to be like that, because you're not a used car salesman. You are a healthcare professional.

Do you have a smooth transition in your talk which naturally leads to what you're offering without it, all of a sudden, becoming gimmicky while you're getting your message across, too? This is the second key to predictability of getting patients from your talks: What are you offering? One of the biggest mistakes most holistic health practitioners make when giving talks is not letting people know what they have to offer. One common approach is the "smile and hope" method. It's easy to feel self-conscious about coming across as being too pushy, and it can feel safer to not inspire people to take you up on what you offer. But as one of my mentors used to always say, it is actually a disservice to not give an offer. If you don't give an offer, you just opened the audience's eyes to new possibility, but you don't let them know how they can get the help they need.

Always give people an offer. Then they can make that decision for themselves about what to do next with their issue. But what do you offer from a talk, and is what you're thinking about offering the best thing to be offering? How are you talking about it so people "get it" without you being too pushy or gimmicky?

Just to show you the importance of having the right offer for a talk, one of my clients is a naturopathic doctor. He loved doing talks, but would rarely get patients from them. People would come up to him and say, "That was a great talk!" He would feel great in the moment and was certain people would call afterwards, but they didn't.

Because he loved doing talks, the first thing we did was get a signature talk together. He came on to a call with me one week thinking he was going to be giving this one offer from his talk. By the end of us talking it through, we decided it needed to be a completely different offer.

That week, he ended up speaking in front of 50 people, and 26 new patients came from it—all of them came in. That's never happened to him before. It just demonstrates the importance of having the right signature talk in place and the right offer for the venue he was speaking at. That is the second key to predictability of getting patients from doing talks.

The third key to predictability of getting patients from doing talks is having the right signature talk in place you can use over and over again, which gives you predictability of getting patients from your talks. That way you don't have to re-invent the wheel. Whenever you speak, you won't have to feel you need to once again create a new talk and spend a lot of time preparing. Instead, if you have a signature talk in place which you can use over and over again, you will have the comfort of knowing what to say. You will get to the point where you know if you do THIS talk in front of THIS kind of an audience, typically THIS number or percentage of patients will come from it. That's when it starts becoming fun!

Let me give you one tip I learned from one of my mentors about how to get to the offer part without feeling like you're being awkward or too salesy all of a sudden. It has to do with what you're saying at the beginning of your talk. One thing you can say after you let your audience know what you're going to cover in the talk today is, "I'm going to give you as much insight as I can in the limited time we have together today, and I'm going to show you how to take this further." At the end of your talk, you can refer to what you said earlier, and it feels like more of a smooth transition. You are more likely to have people curious about what you have to offer even before you reach the end of your talk. That is one tip you can use right away.

When you have a system which works to get people to show up to your talk and get patients, even if you are an introvert, speaking can be a great way to get patients. What does it mean to be an introvert? It is often a misconception that introverts don't talk to people. Typically introverts tend to need more downtime, or like to be by themselves more recharge. Extroverts typically prefer to be around other people to recharge.

For us introverts, we may not necessarily want to be "out there" all the time. Sometimes extroverts call me, wanting to do three or four talks a week. That can feel exhausting to many of us introverts.

But imagine if you could actually have a structure in place where you could give just one talk a month, and that's it; you're done for the month. That's the system you've been learning from today. You can do fewer talks and actually get more patients if you know what you're doing.

To summarize so far, the first key to predictability is to be strategic about who you are speaking to. Are you speaking in front of people who really want to hear what you have to say, or are they just curious?

The second key to predictability is to consider what you are offering. Do you currently offer anything from your talk, and is it the best thing to be offering? How are you talking about it so people take you up on it without you feeling awkward or salesy? When is the best time to let people know what you offer? Is it at the end of the talk or is it somewhere else?

The third key to predictability is do you have the right signature talk in place? That way, instead of reinventing the wheel, you can just use one talk over and over again, and it gives you confidence when you do this talk in front of the right audience, you will typically come away with X number of patients. That's how to do this in an introverted way and be booked up with patients each time you speak. The only thing standing between you and a steady flow of patients (or leveraged/automated income coming into your practice) is one talk which converts.

You have a message you want to share. That's why you were drawn to read this book. You're passionate about helping people, but people don't know about what you do. People are suffering right now from only knowing about drugs and surgery. Sometimes people have been dealing with their health issues for years and doctors don't have answers for them. You actually have a key to what could get them better. But without you making your mark, without sharing your approach with more people, they are not going to know about it.

The problem is many of us think we have time. We think, "Oh, we'll do that later," or, "We'll get that going later." But the truth is we never know how much time we have. That was impressed upon me deeply with what happened to my dad. My dad had a lot of influence on me even though I did not have pleasant memories of him being critical of my talks. He ended up getting Stage IV colon cancer at a young age and filed for bankruptcy. He passed away before his 55th birthday and it happened so fast. I remember my dad used to talk about traveling or doing other things after retirement. He would think, "I'll have time when....." We always think we have time, but the truth is our time here is limited and you were put on this planet to make an impact. You were meant to be sharing what you know to be true with people and making your mark on the world. What are you waiting for?

How to Fill Up Your Schedule with Patients

You may either have a desire to be speaking but you're not sure where to start, or maybe you've done talks before, but it's been disappointing. You're tired of being disappointed because you feel like you have so much to offer. If only more people would know about you and work with you, then you could make a bigger difference.

Or you might be in a place in your practice where you're already really busy in your practice and there's only one of you to go around. You've hit a plateau you can't seem to get past. As you grow, you can't imagine having to work more. Imagine if you actually had money coming in without always having to be at the office. What would that be like for you? When you're reaching more and more people at once, you're helping a lot more people than you possibly could just 1-on-1. And you don't have to see more patients one-on-one when you have a business model which brings in another stream of income from speaking or offering leveraged online or group programs.

I decided to make available to you the opportunity to book a free 6-Figure Speaking Breakthrough Strategy Session. We're going to take a deeper look at the biggest frustrations in your practice right now and how you can have a makeover of your practice through speaking. What's that overall strategic plan for you and what's the next most strategic step to take to have a six-figure or seven-figure makeover of your practice through speaking? In that way, you could feel more comfortable and confident with having a plan in place which can bring in more patients or automated income each time you speak.

Go to **www.OneTalkaMonthBook.com/bonuses**. You will not only get the opportunity to book a six-figure speaking breakthrough strategy session, but you will also get the *Top 10 Best Places to Speak* and *Get Patients* quick start guide and instant access to the Speak and Get Patients Factor Quiz so you can get started with that immediately.

Imagine if you started getting seen as a go-to practitioner, as a go-to expert in your area. You're going to be more in-demand and people will actually come to you. Instead of feeling frustrated by people not knowing about you, have an approach in place that works and brings in patients or another stream of income consistently.

When my client, Dr. C Barnes, first came to me she only had brought in $500 that month and had to borrow money from her parents. Three months later, she was at a place where she was making $5,000 a month. Another client of mine had a fairly successful practice that had stalled in growth. He liked doing talks but they weren't bringing new patients through his door. We worked on getting his signature talk in place and added an offer. His first signature talk in front of 50 people brought in 26 new patients using the 6-Figure Speaking System for Introverts structures. Imagine having a system which gives you that kind of predictability over and over again. All you need to do is rinse and repeat, so you can just focus on helping people and waking up the planet.

Go ahead and go to **www.OneTalkaMonthBook.com/bonuses** to apply for your session and receive all the bonuses. It is my gift to you, and then we'll be in touch with you about your session. Let's give you invaluable insight into your practice and start getting you known. Imagine it starting to become fun to do talks, attract more patients you enjoy working with, and even make passive income through speaking. I'm excited to help you and can't wait to get you going here, so apply for your session now and look forward to seeing you on the session.

Here's How to Do One Talk a Month and Fill up Your Schedule with Patients...

Do you wish you had an easier way of getting more patients? Or is your practice busy and you aren't able to see more patients, but you're not sure how to grow?

Speaking is one of the fastest ways to educate more people about what you do and start getting seen as a go-to practitioner in your community. There's nothing faster than showing up, speaking on a topic, and getting more patients in one hour than you would from a month of networking if you know what you're doing.

Discover a proven system to bring in new patients without having to spend money on advertising or do a lot of marketing. If you love to teach and want to monetize it, go to www.OneTalkaMonthBook.com/quickstart.

Step 1: Decide the best topic to speak on and what to offer your audience, without being awkward or salesy.

Step 2: Learn how to fill up your own talks, or get your foot in the door for speaking engagements. Get invited to speak at coveted speaking opportunities.

Step 3: Create a compelling talk which brings in patients, or turn those talks into passive income so you leverage your time and skills.

Step 4: Start making a name for yourself and wake up the planet by speaking!

Most DCs, LAcs, NDs, holistic MDs/DOs don't like to sell or market themselves, but love educating and teaching. Using the 6-Figure Speaking System for Introverts, you can fill your practice with just one talk a month.

If you'd like us to help, go to: **www.OneTalkaMonth.com/quickstart** to get started.